Pretty Butter Board Recipes

Spectacularly Comforting Butter Boards That'll Warm Your Heart

BY

Jasper Whitethorne

Licensing Notes

Table of Contents

Introduction

Butter boards are much cheaper than cheese and charcuterie boards, and we are loving them all through.

Scanning through the internet and seeing all the beautiful creations people make of butter boards, only pushes us to explore this space. And as we do, it seems good to share our recipes with you.

From floral, cultural, sweet, spicy, fruity, and you name it concepts, butter boards are truly a better way to enjoy butter with lesser cost and quicker time.

Can we talk about how pretty they are too? We think butter boards are an easier way to get started on food boards if you're a beginner.

So to help you with that, these are thirty adorable butter boards for your enjoyment.

1. Garlic Butter Board

Enjoy a rich garlic and parsley butter spread topped with bacon and fried garlic.

Prep Time: 3 mins

Serves: 4+

Ingredients:

For the butter:

- 2 sticks butter, at room temperature
- 1 garlic clove, finely minced
- ¼ chopped fresh parsley

Toppings:

- 3 streaky bacon rashers, finely chopped and cooked
- 2 garlic cloves, thinly sliced and fried
- Sea salt flakes to taste

Instructions:

Mix the butter, garlic, and parsley in a bowl until the butter is a little more softened but not melty.

Spread the butter in a spiral manner or your preferred design on a serving board.

Dress the toppings on the butter, making sure to spread them out evenly.

Serve at room temperature with crusty bread or crackers.

2. Goat Cheese Butter Board with Prosciutto and Figs

A perfect treat for a mini house party.

Prep Time: 3 mins

Serves: 4+

Ingredients:

For the goat cheese butter:

- 4 oz salted butter, softened
- 4 oz goat cheese, softened

Toppings:

- ¼ cup fig jam or preserves
- 2 slices prosciutto
- 4 figs, sliced
- ¼ cup baby arugula
- 2 tbsp walnuts, chopped
- ¼ tsp red pepper flakes
- Flaky salt and black pepper to taste
- 2 tbsp balsamic glaze
- Fresh rosemary or thyme for garnish

Instructions:

Mix the butter and goat cheese in a bowl until a little more softened but not melty.

Spread the butter in a spiral manner or your preferred design on a serving board.

Dress the toppings on the butter, making sure to spread them out evenly.

Serve at room temperature with crusty bread or crackers.

3. Zesty Chive and Chili Butter Board

It is lemony, earthy, and packs some spice.

Prep Time: 3 mins

Serves: 4+

Ingredients:

For the butter:

- 2 tbsp olive oil
- 2 tbsp garlic oil
- 2 sticks unsalted butter, softened
- 1 orange, zested
- 1 lemon, zested

Toppings:

- 1 ½ tbsp thinly sliced chives
- 1 tbsp torn dill sprigs
- 1 tbsp flaky sea salt
- 1 tsp crushed red pepper flakes
- ½ cup crushed nuts of choice
- 3 tbsp honey for drizzling

Instructions:

Mix the butter ingredients in a bowl until the butter is a little more softened but not melty.

Spread the butter in a spiral manner or your preferred design on a serving board.

Dress the toppings on the butter, making sure to spread them out evenly.

Serve at room temperature with crusty bread or crackers.

4. Cinnamon Honey Butter Board

A yummy dessert spread for biscuits, cakes, fruits, etc.

Prep Time: 3 mins

Serves: 4+

Ingredients:

For the butter:

- 2 sticks butter, softened
- ¼ cup honey, divided
- 1 tsp cinnamon, divided

Toppings:

Instructions:

Mix the butter and half each of the honey and cinnamon in a bowl until a little more softened but not melty.

Spread the butter in a spiral manner or your preferred design on a serving board.

Mix the remaining honey and cinnamon, and drizzle on the butter.

Serve at room temperature with crusty bread or crackers.

5. Spicy Butter Board

In for some heat? This simple spread will satisfy you well.

Prep Time: 3 mins

Serves: 4+

Ingredients:

For the butter:

- 2 sticks unsalted butter, softened

Toppings:

- 1 tsp paprika
- 1 tsp red chili flakes
- 2 tsp hot honey
- 1 pinch flaky salt

Instructions:

Mix the butter in a bowl until a little more softened but not melty.

Spread the butter in a spiral manner or your preferred design on a serving board.

Sprinkle the toppings on the butter, making sure to spread them out evenly.

Serve at room temperature with crusty bread or crackers.

6. Lemon Butter Board

A simple lemon butter display with thyme for character and extra flavor.

Prep Time: 3 mins

Serves: 4+

Ingredients:

For the butter:

- 2 sticks butter, softened
- 1 tsp roasted garlic seasoning
- 1 tsp lemon zest

Toppings:

- 2 tsp fresh thyme leaves
- 1 tsp lemon zest
- 2 tsp black pepper

Instructions:

Mix the butter, garlic seasoning, and lemon zest in a bowl until a little more softened but not melty.

Spread the butter in a spiral manner or your preferred design on a serving board.

Sprinkle the toppings on the butter, making sure to spread them out evenly.

Serve at room temperature with crusty bread or crackers.

7. Pecan and Bacon Jam Butter Board

A pretty spread featuring sweet smokiness and nuttiness.

Prep Time: 3 mins

Serves: 4+

Ingredients:

For the butter:

- 2 sticks butter, softened

Toppings:

- 1 tsp date nectar or honey
- 2 tbsp apple maple bacon jam
- ⅓ cup candied pecans, chopped
- Edible flower for garnish

Instructions:

Mix the butter in a bowl until a little more softened but not melty.

Spread the butter in a spiral manner or your preferred design on a serving board.

Dress the toppings on the butter, making sure to spread them out evenly.

Serve at room temperature with crusty bread or crackers.

8. Apple Cider Butter Board

A cheat way to have your apple cider vinegar without a painful drink in the morning.

Prep Time: 3 mins

Serves: 4+

Ingredients:

For the butter:

- 2 sticks butter, softened

Toppings:

- ¼ cup apple cider fruit spread
- A pinch flaky sea salt or to taste
- ½ cup pumpkin seeds
- 2 tbsp fresh rosemary leaves
- 2 tbsp fresh thyme leaves

Instructions:

Mix the butter in a bowl until a little more softened but not melty.

Spread the butter in a spiral manner or your preferred design on a serving board.

Dress the toppings on the butter, making sure to spread them out evenly.

Serve at room temperature with crusty bread or crackers.

9. Snacktime Peanut Butter Board

Make this peanut butter board for you and the kids' snacktime.

Prep Time: 3 mins

Serves: 4+

Ingredients:

For the butter:

- 2 cups creamy peanut butter

Toppings:

- 1 cup M&M candies
- 1 cup chocolate wafer cookies
- 1 cup vanilla wafer cookies
- 1 cup assorted fun size chocolate bars, halved

Instructions:

Mix the peanut butter in a bowl until a little more softened but not melty.

Spread the peanut butter in a spiral manner or your preferred design on a serving board.

Dress the toppings on the butter, making sure to spread them out evenly.

Serve at room temperature with crusty bread or crackers.

10. Pear and Honey Butter Board

Quite comforting and perfect as a rustic romantic treat.

Prep Time: 3 mins

Serves: 4+

Ingredients:

For the butter:

- 2 sticks butter, softened

Toppings:

- 1 to 2 pears, chopped or shaved
- A handful of walnuts, chopped
- Honey for drizzling
- Microgreens for garnish

Instructions:

Mix the butter in a bowl until a little more softened but not melty.

Spread the butter in a spiral manner or your preferred design on a serving board.

Dress the toppings on the butter, making sure to spread them out evenly.

Serve at room temperature with crusty bread or crackers.

11. Berry and Walnut Butter Board

Berry and nuts on butter? Super delicious.

Prep Time: 3 mins

Serves: 4+

Ingredients:

For the butter:

- 2 sticks butter, softened

Toppings:

- 5 to 8 strawberries, hulled and sliced
- ¼ cup fresh blueberries
- ¼ cup chopped walnuts
- 1 tbsp honey
- 2 tsp sea salt
- 1 tbsp mint leaves

Instructions:

Mix the butter in a bowl until a little more softened but not melty.

Spread the butter in a spiral manner or your preferred design on a serving board.

Dress the toppings on the butter, making sure to spread them out evenly.

Serve at room temperature with crusty bread or crackers.

12. Holiday Butter Board

Make this butter board for the entire family and guests during the holidays.

Prep Time: 3 mins

Serves: 4+

Ingredients:

For the butter:

- 2 sticks butter, softened

Toppings:

- 1 tsp fresh orange zest
- ¼ cup cranberry sauce or jam
- 2 tsp minced fresh rosemary
- 3 tbsp pecans, chopped
- 2 tbsp honey
- ½ tsp flaky sea salt

Instructions:

Mix the butter in a bowl until a little more softened but not melty.

Spread the butter in a spiral manner or your preferred design on a serving board.

Dress the toppings on the butter, making sure to spread them out evenly.

Serve at room temperature with crusty bread or crackers.

13. Christmas Butter Board

How perfect is this butter board for Christmas? It is delightful, we must say.

Prep Time: 3 mins

Serves: 4+

Ingredients:

For the butter:

- 2 sticks butter, softened

Toppings:

- ½ cups figs, finely chopped
- ¼ cup roasted garlic cloves
- 1 tbsp fresh orange zest
- 2 tbsp fresh rosemary
- 2 tbsp fresh thyme leaves
- ⅛ cup honey
- ¼ cup dried cranberries or pomegranate arils

Instructions:

Mix the butter in a bowl until a little more softened but not melty.

Spread the butter in a spiral manner or your preferred design on a serving board.

Dress the toppings on the butter, making sure to spread them out evenly.

Serve at room temperature with crusty bread or crackers.

14. Baklava Butter Board

Deconstructed baklava on a butter board and be amazed at how yummy and better the taste gets.

Prep Time: 3 mins

Serves: 4+

Ingredients:

For the butter:

- 2 sticks butter, softened

Toppings:

- ⅓ cup toasted walnuts, roughly chopped
- ⅓ cup toasted pistachios, roughly chopped
- 3 tbsp honey
- ½ tsp ground cinnamon
- Sea salt flakes to taste

Instructions:

Mix the butter in a bowl until a little more softened but not melty.

Spread the butter in a spiral manner or your preferred design on a serving board.

Dress the toppings on the butter, making sure to spread them out evenly.

Serve at room temperature with crusty bread or crackers.

15. Butter Board with Roasted Garlic and Parmesan

Butter, roasted garlic, and Parmesan always work excellently together. This savory butter board is perfect with charcuterie too.

Prep Time: 3 mins

Serves: 4+

Ingredients:

For the butter:

- 2 sticks butter, softened

Toppings:

- 2 tbsp roasted garlic, slightly smashed
- 1 tbsp shaved aged Parmesan cheese
- 3 to 4 fresh basil leaves, cut chiffonade style

Instructions:

Mix the butter in a bowl until a little more softened but not melty.

Spread the butter in a spiral manner or your preferred design on a serving board.

Dress the toppings on the butter, making sure to spread them out evenly.

Serve at room temperature with crusty bread or crackers.

16. Butter Board with Dried Fruits and Honeycomb

You get a balance of sweetness, herbiness, and savoriness from each bite.

Prep Time: 3 mins

Serves: 4+

Ingredients:

For the butter:

- 2 sticks butter, softened

Toppings:

- Honey for drizzling
- 1 to 2 tbsp fresh lemon zest
- 1 to 2 cups sliced dried fruits, strawberries, tangerines, etc.
- ½ cup honeycomb, broken into pieces
- Coarse sea salt to taste
- Chopped fresh rosemary sprigs for garnish

Instructions:

Mix the butter in a bowl until a little more softened but not melty.

Spread the butter in a spiral manner or your preferred design on a serving board.

Dress the toppings on the butter, making sure to spread them out evenly.

Serve at room temperature with crusty bread or crackers.

17. Sweet, Smoky, and Spicy Butter Board

If you love some heat, this butter board will please you well. It is spicy and perfectly savoury.

Prep Time: 3 mins

Serves: 4+

Ingredients:

For the butter:

- 2 sticks butter, softened
- ½ tsp sriracha

Toppings:

- ¼ cup sweet chili sauce
- ¼ cup cooked crumbled bacon
- ¼ cup edibles flower petals for garnish

Instructions:

Mix the butter and sriracha in a bowl until a little more softened but not melty.

Spread the butter in a spiral manner or your preferred design on a serving board.

Dress the toppings on the butter, making sure to spread them out evenly.

Serve at room temperature with crusty bread or crackers.

18. Creamy Jalapeno Popper Board

Deconstruct jalapeno poppers on a butter board and enjoy it more comfortably.

Prep Time: 3 mins

Serves: 4+

Ingredients:

For the base:

- 1 cup softened cream cheese

Toppings:

- ¼ cup finely chopped jalapeños, ribs and seeds removed
- ½ cup sweet pepper jelly
- ¼ cup butter-toasted breadcrumbs

Instructions:

Mix the cream cheese in a bowl until a little more softened.

Spread the cream cheese in a spiral manner or your preferred design on a serving board.

Spread on the sweet pepper jelly and sprinkle on the jalapenos and breadcrumbs.

Serve at room temperature with tortilla chips.

19. Hummus "Butter" Board

There isn't any butter here but this recipe explores how lovely you can serve hummus other than in a bowl.

Prep Time: 3 mins

Serves: 4+

Ingredients:

- 2 cups prepared hummus
- ¼ cup pesto (optional)
- ¼ cup sun-dried or chopped tomatoes
- ¼ cup finely diced cucumber
- ¼ cup black olive slices
- 1 tbsp grated lemon zest
- 8 to 10 basil leaves, torn or chopped fresh dill
- 2 tbsp garlic-infused olive oil
- ¼ cup pine nuts
- ¼ cup crumbled feta cheese

Instructions:

Spread the hummus in a spiral manner or your preferred design on a serving board.

Spread on the pesto, if using and top with the remaining ingredients.

Serve with pita bread.

20. Everything Bagel "Butter" Board

The spreading element here is cream cheese for a perfect Everything Bagel take that is right for your bagels.

Prep Time: 3 mins

Serves: 4+

Ingredients:

For the base:

- 1 cup softened cream cheese

Toppings:

- 2 to 3 tbsp Everything Bagel seasoning
- ¼ cup flaked smoked salmon or lox
- 1 tbsp drained capers
- Small fresh dill sprigs for garnish

Instructions:

Mix the cream cheese in a bowl until a little more softened.

Spread the cream cheese in a spiral manner or your preferred design on a serving board.

Sprinkle on the Everything Bagel seasoning and dress the remaining toppings on the cream cheese, making sure to spread them out evenly.

Serve at room temperature with mini bagels.

21. Hibiscus and Lavender Honey Butter Board

Enjoy this floral butter board that is refreshing and perfect for spring.

Prep Time: 3 mins

Serves: 4+

Ingredients:

For the butter:

- 1 tsp finely grated lime zest
- 2 sticks butter, softened

Toppings:

- 1 tbsp dried food-grade lavender
- ¼ cup dried, candied hibiscus flowers, chopped
- 2 tbsp lavender honey
- ¼ cup chopped pecans

Instructions:

Mix the butter and lemon zest in a bowl until a little more softened but not melty.

Spread the butter in a spiral manner or your preferred design on a serving board.

Dress the toppings on the butter, making sure to spread them out evenly.

Serve at room temperature with crusty baguette or crackers.

22. Caramelized Onion Butter Board

Loaded with sweetened onions, you can spread some of the butter on the steak and it will be delicious.

Prep Time: 3 mins

Serves: 4+

Ingredients:

For the butter:

- 2 sticks butter, softened
- 2 tbsp roasted garlic cloves, mashed
- 2 tbsp caramelized onions
- 1 tbsp grated Parmesan cheese

Toppings:

- 1 tbsp grated Parmesan cheese
- ¼ cup caramelized onions
- 2 tsp dukkah seasoning
- Handful freshly picked basil leaves for garnish

Instructions:

Blitz the butter ingredients in a food processor or until the butter is a little more softened and onions broken up.

Spread the butter in a spiral manner or your preferred design on a serving board.

Dress the toppings on the butter, making sure to spread them out evenly.

Serve at room temperature with crusty bread or crackers.

23. Fig and Walnut Butter Board

Fig and walnut are perfect for butter boards. Why not try out the blend of honey tastes and nuttiness today?

Prep Time: 3 mins

Serves: 4+

Ingredients:

For the butter:

- 2 sticks butter, softened

Toppings:

- 2 tbsp honey + extra for drizzling
- 2 to 3 tbsp fig jam
- A handful of roasted walnuts
- 2 to 3 figs, quartered
- Fresh thyme sprigs for garnish
- A pinch flaky sea salt

Instructions:

Mix the butter in a bowl until a little more softened but not melty.

Spread the butter in a spiral manner or your preferred design on a serving board.

Dress the toppings on the butter, making sure to spread them out evenly.

Serve at room temperature with crusty bread or crackers.

24. Mushroom and Onion Butter Board

Recreate your standard mushroom sauce on a board and you have a delicious appetizer to pass around.

Prep Time: 3 mins

Serves: 4+

Ingredients:

For the butter:

- 2 sticks butter, softened

Toppings:

- 2 cups sliced mushrooms, sauteed
- 1 medium red onion, thinly sliced and sauteed
- 2 tbsp roasted garlic cloves, mashed
- Chopped fresh chives, rosemary, and thyme for garnish
- Kosher salt and black pepper to taste

Instructions:

Mix the butter in a bowl until a little more softened but not melty.

Spread the butter in a spiral manner or your preferred design on a serving board.

Dress the toppings on the butter, making sure to spread them out evenly.

Serve at room temperature with crusty bread or crackers.

25. Chili and Sun-Dried Tomato Butter Board

This butter board has subtle Mediterranean vibes to it and we love it.

Prep Time: 3 mins

Serves: 4+

Ingredients:

For the butter:

- 2 sticks butter, softened

Toppings:

- 2 tbsp chili paste
- ¼ to ½ cup sun-dried tomatoes, chopped
- Honey for drizzling
- Flakey sea salt to taste
- Fresh basil leaves as garnish

Instructions:

Mix the butter in a bowl until a little more softened but not melty.

Spread the butter in a spiral manner or your preferred design on a serving board.

Dress the toppings on the butter, making sure to spread them out evenly.

Serve at room temperature with crusty bread.

26. Greek Feta Board

Wouldn't you love to indulge in this Greek-rich butter board?

Prep Time: 3 mins

Serves: 4+

Ingredients:

- 1 (8 oz) block feta cheese
- 2 tbsp plain yogurt
- 2 mini cucumbers chopped small
- 10 cherry tomatoes, halved
- ½ of a sweet green pepper, diced
- A few thin slices of red onion
- A small handful of olives
- A tiny pinch of salt
- Olive oil for drizzling
- Dried oregano for garnish

Instructions:

Whip the feta and yogurt in a bowl until smooth.

Spread the whipped feta in a spiral manner or your preferred design on a serving board.

Dress the remaining ingredients on the feta, making sure to spread them out evenly.

Serve at room temperature with pita bread.

27. Pistachio Halva Butter Board

Crumble some halva on a butter board with some pistachios and enjoy this yummy Middle Eastern snack in a different way.

Prep Time: 3 mins

Serves: 4+

Ingredients:

For the butter:

- 2 sticks butter, softened

Toppings:

- 2 to 3 tbsp sour cream
- Honey for drizzling
- ¼ cup crumbled halva
- A handful of toasted pistachios
- Edible dried roses for garnish

Instructions:

Mix the butter in a bowl until a little more softened but not melty.

Spread the butter in a spiral manner or your preferred design on a serving board.

Dress the toppings on the butter, making sure to spread them out evenly.

Serve at room temperature with crusty bread or crackers.

28. Persian Feta Board

The color invites you in an instant and the taste keeps you locked in.

Prep Time: 3 mins

Serves: 4+

Ingredients:

For the base:

- 8 oz feta cheese
- 3 tbsp Greek yogurt

Toppings:

- 1 tbsp extra virgin olive oil
- 1 small tomato, finely diced
- 1 Persian cucumber, finely diced
- A handful of walnuts
- 2 radishes, thinly sliced
- Handful fresh mint leaves for garnish

Instructions:

Whip the feta and yogurt in a bowl until smooth.

Spread the whipped feta in a spiral manner or your preferred design on a serving board.

Dress the remaining ingredients on the feta, making sure to spread them out evenly.

Serve at room temperature with pita bread.

29. Sparkly Christmas Butter Board

Quite simple on the ingredients but perfectly pretty.

Prep Time: 3 mins

Serves: 4+

Ingredients:

For the butter:

- 2 sticks butter, softened

Toppings:

- 1 tbsp flaky sea salt
- 1 to 2 tbsp honey
- ¼ to ½ cup pistachios, chopped
- ¼ to ½ cup dried cranberries

Instructions:

Mix the butter in a bowl until a little more softened but not melty.

Spread the butter in a spiral manner or your preferred design on a serving board.

Dress the toppings on the butter, making sure to spread them out evenly.

Serve at room temperature with crusty bread or crackers.

30. Apricot and Goat Cheese Butter Board

It is a merge of many different elements and colors, and the taste pleases you just as it looks.

Prep Time: 3 mins

Serves: 4+

Ingredients:

For the base:

- 1 cup soft goat cheese
- 2 tbsp cream cheese, softened
- *Optional to have butter at the base*

Toppings:

- Plain or seasoned honey for drizzling
- ¼ cup dried apricot
- Edible flowers for garnish

Instructions:

Whip the goat cheese and cream cheese in a bowl until smooth.

Spread the whipped goat cheese in a spiral manner or your preferred design on a serving board.

Dress the remaining ingredients on the cheese, making sure to spread them out evenly.

Serve at room temperature with pita bread.

Conclusion

Which butter board are you trying out first?

As with many things, butter boards are easily tweakable to fit just about any design that you like. There isn't any fuss with making them but expect a beautiful symphony of how the flavors meld in your mouth.

These butter boards are just a handful of what you could possibly be fantastically creating. We hope you'd get into making many more types.

Author's Afterthought

Thank you!

Experiencing the heavens is how I feel, and it's all because of you, my dear reader, for helping me reach this point. I crafted this book specifically for you, and it holds great significance to me that you discovered and embraced it. Amidst the numerous books with similar content, you chose this one. These Goosebumps are truly exhilarating.

There's one additional favor I'd like to ask of you. Others are searching for the perfect book to download and enjoy, and your thoughts might be the nudge they require. Moreover, I'm eager to learn your opinions on the book as well. Your feedback will be incredibly beneficial.

Once more, thank you.

Jasper Whitethorne